Gold Beach

The D-day landing beach code-named « Gold » by the planners of Operation Overlord spanned ac[...] Rivière at Ver sur Mer in the east to the foot of the cliff at Saint Côme to the west. Its name was give[...] for the D-day invasion by General Montgomery.
- 50th Infantry Division (Tyne and Tees),
- 8th Armoured Brigade in support,
- 7th Armoured Brigade (the Desert Rats) whose task would be to push past Bayeux to reach the objective of Villers Bocage, 30 kilometres to the south.

Each of these experienced units, along with the support of engineers and beach organization personnel, had all contributed to Monty's* prestigious victory over Rommel at El Alamein two years earlier. Those veterans of North Africa « still had sand in their boots » and that is why Gold, the colour of sand, was chosen after their landing in Italy in 1943 as the name of their next (and last) invasion beach. Facing an infantry battalion from the Wehrmacht's 716th Infantry Division and some artillery elements of the Kriegsmarine, the beach would be stormed in four sectors :
« ITEM » in front of the resistance nests WN38 and WN37 at Asnelles / Puits d'Hérode,
« JIG » in front of WN36 at Meuvaines / Les Roquettes,
« KING » in front of the WN35 bastion at Hable de Heurtot, WN33 at La Rivière and WN34 at Mont Fleury, with the lighthouse and radio mast at Ver sur Mer in the distance,
« LOVE » was not one of the landing sectors on Gold beach.

The coastal area between Ver and Asnelles had been flooded by the enemy, and medium gun batteries had been set up inland at Meuvaines, Ryes and Crépon. A battalion of men from the 352nd Infantry Division sat waiting in reserve. To the west, on the coast at Saint Côme de Fresné, another 105 mm gun battery concentrated its fire along ITEM sector, thereby protecting the radar station on the cliff at Arromanches which was manned by Navy troops. The fishing port at Arromanches was defended by a half-company of infantry and three guns « from another war ». No frontal attack was expected there and the 300 residents were chased out of their waterfront homes. Arromanches was captured from behind at 6:30 pm by soldiers of the 1st Battalion, Royal Hampshire Regiment.

The vast expanse of fine sand, which at low tide stretched one kilometre out to sea, was attacked at 7:30 am on June 6th 1944 at narrow sectors, which allowed 231st and 69th Infantry Brigades to concentrate on less heavily-defended areas. The amphibious tanks of the Sherwood Rangers and 4/7th Dragoon Guards took on the hidden anti-tank guns while the AVREs (Armoured Vehicle Royal Engineers) attacked the blockhouse and the minesweeping flail tanks cleared the way for the Beach Groups to secure the exits (6th Battalion, the Border Regiment and 2nd Battalion, the Hertfordshire Regiment). An hour later, thanks to good aerial reconnaissance and supporting naval artillery fire, XXX Corps had smashed through the Atlantic Wall in the three planned spots, except at La Rivière where the stubborn beach defences around the 88 gun at WN33 held out until 9:30 am. The silencing of the guns at Mont Fleury complemented the British victory at Gold beach, in tandem with the valiant action by Sergeant-Major Stanley Hollis (7th Green Howards) who would earn the only Victoria Cross awarded on D-Day, the highest decoration of the British Empire. Meanwhile, N°.47 Royal Marine Commando landed at Asnelles (Le Hamel) and charged through 13 kilometres of ennemy territory to reach Port en Bessin 36 hours later with 200 casualties. Overwhelmed, the Atlantic Wall began to crack under the tidal wave of British troops now coveting its next theoretical objective, Villers Bocage, which would only be captured… two months later.

* Monty : name given to Montgomery by his men.

Jean-Pierre BENAMOU, Founder of the Bayeux Memorial Museum.
Royalties from this book will be donated to the Royal British Legion, Normandy Calvados Branch.

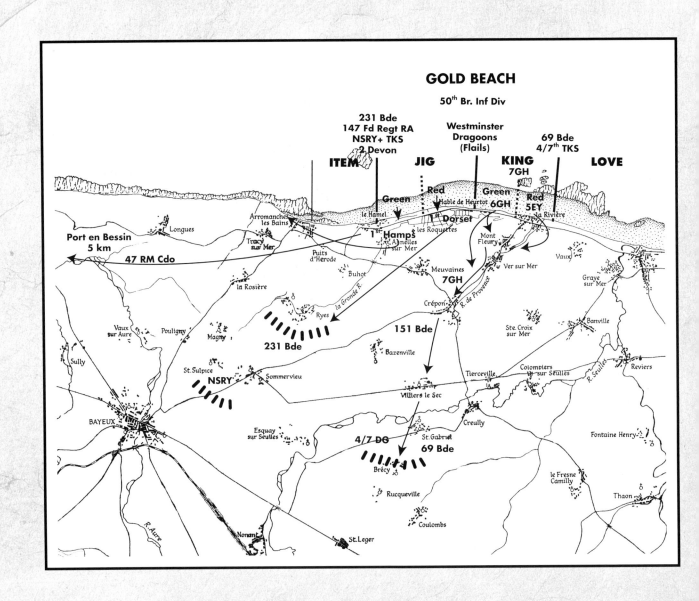

Fonds J.-P. B

Vue d'ensemble, le 6 juin à 16 heures

Secteur King Red sur la plage de La Rivière, depuis un LCT* américain qui achemine les matériels de la 8ème Brigade Blindée, ici pour les chars du 4/7ème Royal Dragoon Guards qui ont appuyé la 69ème Brigade sur Ver sur Mer. La digue a été franchie en plusieurs points par des engins alors que l'Infanterie du 5ème East-Yorks a dû contourner les maisons fortifiées pour prendre la défense à revers. En arrière plan, le Mont Fleury et le phare de Ver sur Mer, pris par le 6ème, puis le 7ème Bataillon des Green Howards à 9 h 30.

*LCT : péniches de débarquements de chars.

Overview, June 6th, 4:00 pm

King Red sector and the beach at La Rivière, as seen from an American LCT* transporting equipment for 8th Armoured Brigade, in this case the tanks of the 4/7th Royal Dragoon Guards in support of 69th Brigade at Ver sur Mer. The sea wall was breached by armoured vehicles in numerous places but infantry of the 5th East Yorks had to go round the fortified houses to take up a defensive position from the rear. In the background, Mont Fleury and the lighthouse at Ver sur Mer are visible, and these were captured by 6th and 7th Battalions, Green Howards, at 9:30 am.

* LCT : Tank landing craft.

Fonds J.-P. B

Après la bataille de la plage King Red, le canon de 88 de La Rivière n'est plus qu'un trophée pour les organisateurs militaires du trafic des plages. Lui-même parfaitement protégé des tirs venus de la mer, il est responsable de la perte du groupe de commandement du 5ème East-Yorkshire et de la destruction de 5 blindés britanniques. Aujourd'hui, il abrite le club de voile de Ver sur Mer et par tempête, résiste spectaculairement à l'assaut des lames.

After the battle on King Red beach, the 88 gun at La Rivière was nothing more than a trophy reminder for the beach organisation personnel directing traffic on the beach. The gun itself had been well-protected from naval fire, and was responsible for casualties among 5th East Yorkshire's command group, and for the destruction of five British armoured vehicles. Today the site is home to the sailing school at Ver sur Mer and the only violence it sees now is the occasional storm.

Fonds J.-P. B.- Photo d'époque - Qualité d'origine.

La plage de La Rivière et les villas murées et évacuées depuis 1943. Elles s'inscrivent dans le système défensif du WN33 avec deux canons légers protégeant la redoute du 88 plus à droite (à l'ouest). Ici, les soldats du 2ème Hertfordshire procèdent au dégagement des obstacles de plage à l'aide d'un bulldozer blindé. Les dommages causés aux maisons sont dûs aux tirs d'artillerie, de chars et d'armes légères.

The beach at La Rivière and the boarded-up villas, vacant since 1943. They were incorporated into the WN33 defence system, which included two light guns which protected the dreadful 88 which stood to the right (to the west). Here, soldiers from the 2nd Hertfordshires clear obstacles from the beach with an armoured bulldozer. Damage to the houses was caused by artillery, tank and light weapon fire.

Fonds J-P. B

A La Rivière, face au Mont Fleury sur la plage Jig Red, débarquement de chars des Rats du désert (7ème DB), qui seront stoppés quatre jours plus tard à Villers Bocage, l'objectif de cette grande unité. Noter la pluie de juin qui gênera considérablement l'acheminement de la logistique et l'aviation de soutien alliée. Prise de la cabine de pilotage du LCT, cette photo nous montre les Shermans du 4ème County of London Yeomanry, les « tireurs d'élite » anglais.

At La Rivière, in front of Mont Fleury on Jig Red sector, tanks of the Desert Rats (7th Armoured Division) come ashore. They would be stopped four days later at Villers Bocage, the unit objective. The wet June weather considerably hampered the efficiency of logistics and allied air support. This photograph, taken from the LCT's wheelhouse, shows the Sherman tanks of the 4th Country of London Yeomanry « sharpshooters ».

ANC

La plage King Green le 6 juin vers 15 heures

Ce très intéressant document montre l'acheminement par péniche légère d'Infanterie LCA, des troupes du 7ème Green Howards de la 69ème Brigade. Les marins sont canadiens, c'est la seconde marée basse du mardi 6 juin et le rendement des mises à terre est excellent. A gauche, le radio-phare de Ver sur Mer et le bois du château. A droite, la maison au parterre arrondi servant de repère à la sortie de la plage King Green. En arrière de la maison, le WN34 Mont Fleury et ses réseaux de tunnels et casemates enterrés pris le matin par le bataillon. Noter la ligne de 13 LCT lourds rangés côte à côte, qui se hisseront sur leurs ancres à marée haute, pour se remettre à flots.

King Green beach, June 6th at around 3:00 pm

This is a fascinating photograph showing the arrival of troops of the 7th Green Howards, 69th Brigade as they exit their LCA landing craft. The sailors in the picture were Canadian, it was low tide on Tuesday June 6th, and the landings were going according to plan. To the left, the radio mast at Ver sur Mer and the wooded area near the château are visible. Behind the house is the Mont Fleury WN34 resistance nest with its tunnel network and buried casemate, which would be captured by the battalion later that morning. Note the row of 13 beached heavy LCTs, waiting for the next high tide to pull away from shore.

Ce Sherman amphibie du 4/7ème Dragoons a déchenillé sur une mine après avoir soutenu East-Yorskshires et Green Howards autour des WN34 Mont Fleury et WN35A Ver sur Mer. Noter le château d'eau et le phare entourés de tranchées en zig-zag.

This amphibious Sherman of the 4/7th Dragoons blew out a track on a mine after having supported the East-Yorkshires and Green Howards in their actions at the Mont Fleury WN34 resistance nest and WN35A at Ver sur Mer. The water tower and the lighthouse are surrounded by zig-zag trenches.

IWM

La sortie de plage du Paisty Ver vue de la maison dominant le plateau de Ver sur Mer. Photo prise le 8 juin alors que débarquent toujours les 3 600 véhicules de la 7ème DB, les « rats du désert » avec chars Cromwell de reconnaissance et chars moyens Sherman. Les véhicules non chenillés suivent la rue de la mer vers La Rivière où le 88 est désormais muet.

Paisty Ver beach exit, as seen from the house atop the plateau at Ver sur Mer. This photograph was taken on June 8th while the 3 600 vehicles belonging to 7th Armoured Division, the « Desert Rats » came ashore, among them Cromwell reconnaissance tanks and medium Sherman tanks. Non-tracked vehicles used the coastal road to La Rivière, the silenced 88 gun no longer posing threat.

IW/M - Photo d'époque - Qualité d'origine.

Les rues étroites de Ver sur Mer se prêtent mal au trafic chargé des véhicules en route vers Crépon. Noter la pompe à essence hors service depuis quatre ans à cause des restrictions, le tout surveillé par la belle tour du 11ème siècle de l'église de Ver sur Mer. Le camion Fordson porte la cocarde de la RAF, l'aérodrome « B3 » de Sainte Croix sur Mer n'est qu'à trois kilomètres.

The narrow streets in Ver sur Mer were not ideal for heavy traffic headed for Crépon. The gas pump had been out of service for the last four years due to rationing. Note the 11th century church tower. The Fordson truck has RAF markings ; B3 airfield at Sainte Croix sur Mer was only three kilometres away.

IWM

Ver sur Mer, 7 juin

Dans la grande rue du village, la circulation est réglementée par la « Military-Police ». Une colonne de fantassins de la 50ᵉᵐᵉ Division Northumbrian, monte en ligne. Le Sherman M4A2 est stoppé, moteur tournant au ralenti ; il pleut, le chef de char a revêtu un ciré, le béret noir du corps blindé vissé sur la tête, le grésillement de la radio de bord lui parvenant par les écouteurs. Les toits sont en bon état, il n'y a pas eu de combats de rues le 6 juin, alors que les fils téléphoniques sont tombés, probablement en raison des manœuvres délicates des gros véhicules.

Ver sur Mer, June 7ᵗʰ

Traffic on the main street in the village was controlled by the Military Police. Here, a column of infantrymen of the 50ᵗʰ Northumbrian) Division marches in file. The M4A2 Sherman sat idling ; it was raining and the tank commander had donned a slicker, all the while keeping his black Armoured Corps beret and headset, through which he listened to the crackling of the radio. The roofs along this street are intact as there was no street fighting here on June 6ᵗʰ. Only the telephone wires have fallen, likely due to the delicate manoeuvring of large vehicles.

IWM

Par la route de Meuvaines qui rejoint la plage Jig autrefois recouverte de la légendaire forêt de Quintefeuille, une colonne de prisonniers allemands découvre la flotte alliée responsable de la logistique, qui traite également des prisonniers de guerre. L'armée pourvoit à leur sécurité et à leur santé, mais la tête de pont en juin est si étroite qu'il n'y a pas de place pour les vastes camps de prisonniers. La mauvaise météo réduisant les ravitaillements, les camps seront constitués en Grande-Bretagne, au Canada et aux USA. Les uniformes sont ceux de la Wehrmacht, à l'exception des cinq derniers soldats qui appartiennent à la 12ème Division Blindée SS Hitler-Jugend.

A column of German prisoners marches along the Meuvaines road that leads to Jig beach, once the site of the legendary Quintefeuille Forest. These soldiers will meet the Allied branch that deals with logistics and prisoners of war. The Army would see to their health and safety, but the bridgehead was still too narrow in June to accomodate large POW camps. Bad weather slowed supply shipments, and as a result camps were set up in Great Britain, Canada and the United States. Most of the prisoners are wearing Wehrmacht uniforms, except for the last five, who belong to the 12th SS Hitler Youth Division.

6 juin, 12 heures

La plage de Meuvaines dite « Cabane des douaniers » où l'infanterie de sécurité des plages (6ᵉᵐᵉ Border) coordonne les débarquements à partir des LCT acheminant les services de la 8ᵉᵐᵉ Brigade Blindée. A gauche, un Sherman amphibie est toujours recouvert de sa jupe de flottaison gonflable. A droite, une chenillette Bren carrier patauge vers le sable sec.

June 6ᵗʰ at noon

The beach at Meuvaines, where infantry troops in charge of beach security (6ᵗʰ Battalion, the Border Regiment) coordinated the landings of LCTs carrying elements of 8ᵗʰ Armoured Brigade. To the left, an amphibious Sherman tank comes ashore, its inflatable flotation skirt still raised. To the right, a tracked Bren carrier makes its way to dry land.

Fonds J.-P. B

Un Liberty Ship est en voie de déchargement par grues et palans directement dans les camions anglais du Royal Army Service Corps. C'est l'été et les enfants d'Asnelles immédiatement libérés le 6 juin, profitent des innombrables pataugeoires creusées par les ancres des navires à marée basse.

Cranes and hoists were used to unload supplies from this Liberty Ship directly into Royal Army Service Corps trucks. In the foreground, recently-liberated children from Asnelles take advantage of the countless wading pools created by the ship anchors at low tide.

IWM

La même plage du Hamel d'Asnelles où débarquèrent le 6 juin à 7 h 30 les 1ers Hampshires de la 231ème Brigade. Sous le soleil de juillet, les lourds LST* acheminent toujours, à pieds secs, les matériels lourds nécessaires aux opérations du XXXème Corps d'Armée. Noter dans le fond à droite, la passerelle de la sortie de plage Jig Red « Les Roquettes ». Un canon Bofors de DCA est positionné sur la dune, la Luftwaffe rôde toujours de nuit.

* LST : Landing Ship Tank, navire de débarquement pour chars.

The same beach at the Hamel in Asnelles, where the 1st Hampshires of 231st Brigade landed at 7:30 am on June 6th. This photograph was taken in the hot July sun, while equipment destined for XXX Army Corps was being unloaded from heavy LSTs. In the background and to the right is the Roquettes beach exit on Jig Red. A Bofor anti-aircraft defense gun guards is set up on the beach to protect against Luftwaffe raids at night.*

* LST : Landing Ship Tank.

IWM

Plage des Roquettes ou Jig Red quelques jours après le D-Day : échouage des LCT transbordant les blindés, chars Sherman filant vers la sortie de plage, ici de la 11ème Division Blindée. A gauche, une colonne logistique de DUKW's et camions de ravitaillement, à droite, verticale, une passerelle du génie. L'élan sur la plage est irrésistible, il s'essouffle pourtant à Cheux pour être stoppé sur l'Odon.

Roquettes beach or « Jig Red » a few days after D-Day : LCTs carrying armoured vehicles have come ashore, and Sherman tanks of 11th Armoured Division file through the beach exit. To the left is a column of supply DUKW's and trucks, and a gangway can be seen to the right. The run up to the beach was irresistible, but it would slow down at Cheux, and come to a halt in front of the Odon river.

La même plage d'assaut du 1er Dorset de la 231ème Brigade, photographiée du WN36 en 1945. On notera le canon antichar de 50 mm mis hors de combat par les blindés spéciaux du Génie soutenant les Dorsets, quelques minutes après 7 h 30. En arrière, la passerelle inutile dressée par le Génie pour marquer la sortie de plage, est toujours en place un an plus tard.

The same beach where the 1st Battalion, Dorset Regiment of 231st Brigade landed - as seen from WN36 in 1945. The 50 mm anti-tank gun was put out of commission by AVREs supporting the Dorsets just after 7:30 am. In the distance, the walkway built by the engineers at the beach exit is still in place.

Fonds J-P. B

La sortie de plage des Roquettes conduit à la route 814 et à Asnelles par la « maison aux chiens ». Jusqu'en 1947, la passerelle qui la marque en sera le témoin figé, jusqu'au passage des ferrailleurs.

The beach exit at Les Roquettes led to route 814 and on to Asnelles via the « dog house ». This walkway remained stuck on that beach until it was removed by scrap merchants.

Fonds J-P. B

La sortie de plage du Hamel en 1945

Alors que la pêche reprend ses droits, même si l'environnement sur Jig Red demeure dangereux. Remarquer le bunker au milieu des villas et maisonnettes fortifiées, pris à revers le 6 juin par les chars des Sherwood Rangers et du Génie Blindé du 82ème Escadron.

Hamel beach exit in 1945

Even though Jig Red was still a dangerous area, fishing soon resumed along the beach. Notice the bunker among the villas and fortified houses. It had been taken from behind on June 6th by the tanks of the Sherwood Rangers and the AVREs of 82nd squadron.

Fonds J-P. B

Sur la plage d'Asnelles en juillet 1944

Cet officier de la Royal Navy semble avoir adopté les enfants de la colonie de vacances d'Asnelles ! Ces derniers posent avec une maman et une grande sœur, devant un camion amphibie DUKW de la marine royale. A la main droite du marin, un garçon arbore fièrement le bâton torsadé de tradition dans la Royal Navy, tandis que son voisin est en col… marin ! Se reconnaîtront-ils ?

On the beach at Asnelles in July 1944

This Royal Navy officer seems to have adopted all of the children from the local summer camp ! Posing here with a mother and older sister, the group stands in front of an amphibious DUKW truck belonging to the Royal Navy. To the sailor's right, a young boy proudly holds the traditional ornate staff of the Royal Navy, and his neighbor wears a sailor suit. Perhaps they might recognize themselves in this photograph ?

ANC

Juin 1944

Une escouade d'infanterie quitte la plage de Meuvaines par la sortie des Roquettes en contournant un poste de contrôle de la Royal Navy marqué par le « White Ensign ». Noter la jeep amphibie et les Liberty Ships de 3 000 tonnes échoués à la dernière marée haute pour débarquer le ravitaillement à « pieds secs ».

June 1944

A section of infantrymen leave the beach at Meuvaines through the Roquettes beach exit, passing a Royal Navy checkpoint designated by a White Ensign flag. Note the amphibious jeep and the beached 3 000- tonne Liberty Ship, ready to unload its cargo onto dry land.

Fonds J-P. B

Photo aérienne prise le 6 novembre 1943

Cliché de caméra automatique oblique du Spitfire de reconnaissance. Ces documents, pris par centaines, ont conduit à une parfaite connaissance théorique des plages d'assaut.

Aerial photograph taken November 6th 1943

This photograph was taken by an automatic sidelong camera mounted on a Spitfire used for reconnaissance. These snapshots, taken by the hundreds, helped to compile a perfect theoretical understanding of the landing beaches.

Fonds J-P. B

Asnelles et le Hamel, 12 avril 1944

Photo aérienne verticale prise par un avion de reconnaissance américain. La mer est pleine et les points d'appui allemands semblent discrets. Le gros bunker abritant un 75 antichars apparaît clairement sur la place du Hamel, ainsi que la batterie du Puits d'Hérode à l'ouest d'Asnelles (à gauche). Les cultures semblent nettes malgré les nombreux agriculteurs prisonniers de guerre retenus en Allemagne.

Asnelles and le Hamel, April 12th 1944

This vertical aerial photograph was taken by an American reconnaissance aircraft. The tide was high and the German strongpoints seem less evident. The large bunker housing a 75 mm anti-tank gun can clearly be seen at le Hamel, and so can the battery at Puits d'Hérode to the west of Asnelles (to the left). The fields look well tended, despite the fact that many farmers had been sent off to prison camps in Germany.

Fonds J.-P. B

Le long mur antichars d'Asnelles s'achève au point d'appui WN37 dont on aperçoit le canon sous blockhaus. Epais de 90 cm de béton armé et hauts de 2 mètres 50, ces murs étaient couverts de buissons de barbelés avec un poste de mitrailleuses en enfilade. Ces murs barraient les voies d'approche naturelle des plages.

The long anti-tank wall at Asnelles extended all the way to WN37, and the blockhouse and gun can be seen here. Made of 90 cm thick fortified concrete, the walls were 2.5 metres high and covered with bundles of barbed wire. A machine gun emplacement provided enfilade fire. These walls barred all natural access to the beaches.

USIS

Après les combats du matin au Hamel, le 6 juin, des tankistes du Westminster Dragoons vérifient l'efficacité du tir de leurs chars Sherman « Crabs » qui, s'ils sont équipés d'un fléau-démineur, n'en possèdent pas moins un canon de 75 dont les impacts apparaissent à gauche. A droite débute le mur antichars du WN37.

After a morning of fighting on the beach at Hamel on June 6th, a tank crew from the Westminster Dragoons examines the accuracy of the Sherman « Crab » tanks, equipped with minesweeping flails and 75 mm guns. The impact can be seen to the left of the photograph. To the right, the anti-tank wall at WN37 is barely visible.

Fonds J.-P. B

Dernière photo d'Asnelles avec informations ultimes notées à la date du 14 mai 1944. Le village d'Asnelles s'étend perpendiculairement à la côte où apparaissent les points d'appui WN37 du Hamel avec 4 canons, à droite, et le WN36 de la « Cabane aux douaniers » à gauche, avec 3 pièces en cuves, rapidement neutralisés par les Hampshires et les Dorsets de la 231ème Bde. Les mines sont omniprésentes aux sorties de plages, notées en U inversés, aux Roquettes et à Asnelles.

The last reconnaissance photograph taken of Asnelles, dated May 14th 1944. The village of Asnelles was perpendicular to the coast and defended to the right by the WN37 strongpoint with its four guns, and to the left by WN36, the « Customs house » with three protected guns which were rapidly neutralized by the Hampshire and Dorset Regiments of 231st Brigade. Mines were plentiful - especially at the beach exits - and are represented here by the upside-down « U » shapes at les Roquettes and Asnelles.

IWM

Le Hamel, 6 juin, 10 heures

Après avoir contourné les réseaux fortifiés du point d'appui WN37, les chars des Notts and Sherwood Rangers (Robin des bois) et troupes antichars des Northumberland Hussards, s'infiltrent vers Asnelles en direction de Ryes. Les échappements aériens sont démontés et abandonnés, les Hampshires prennent, eux, la route d'Arromanches qui tombera ce même soir.

Le Hamel, June 6th, 10:00 am

After bypassing the fortified network of the WN37 strongpoint, tanks of the Nottinghamshire (Sherwood Rangers) Yeomanry and anti-tank crews of the Northumberland Hussars advance through Asnelles towards Ryes. After dismantling the tanks' flotation devices, the Hampshires headed towards Arromanches, which was captured that same evening.

Fonds J.-P. B

La plage du Hamel où débarquèrent les 1ers Hampshires soutenus par les chars amphibies (DD Tanks) de la Nottinghamshire Yeomanry, face au solide point d'appui WN37 qui tombera à 9 heures.

The beach at Hamel where the 1st Hampshires came ashore, supported by the DD amphibious tanks of the Nottinghamshire Yeomanry, in front of the WN37 strongpoint which was neutralized at 9:00 am.

Fonds J.-P. B

Les Hampshires furent surpris de voir, au cœur du combat, « surgir des Français qui semblaient aller " au lait " comme si ce qui se passait autour d'eux ne les concernait pas » ! Nous voyons ici la rue littorale entre le bunker au canon de 50, et le 75 qui doit être derrière le photographe. Un char Petard du 82ème Escadron d'assaut lui règlera son compte, soutenu par les flails des Westminster Dragoons. L'ensemble défensif dit du « Sanatorium » tombera à 9 h 30, traversé par les artilleurs motorisés de l'Essex Yeomanry. Leurs canons automoteurs devront largement contourner le fossé antichars d'Asnelles en forme de V, long de 1,5 km.

In the thick of the fighting, the Hampshires were astounded to see French people going about their business as if nothing was amiss. Shown here is the stretch of coastal road between one bunker housing a 50 mm gun and another housing a 75 mm gun, which would have been behind the photographer. A Petard tank from 82nd Assault Squadron put it out of commission with help from the flails of the Westminster Dragoons. The defensive area know as the « Sanatorium » fell at 9:30 am, allowing the mechanized artillery of the Essex Yeomanry to cross through it. The regiment's self-propelled guns had to take the long way round the 1.5 km, V-shaped anti-tank ditch at Asnelles.

IWM

Les bérets verts de la Marine Royale du 47ème Commando s'élancent sur le Hamel deux heures après l'assaut des 231ème Brigade et 8ème Brigade Blindée légèrement armés mais rompus à la course et aux marches forcées ; leur objectif est à 13 kilomètres d'Asnelles, Port en Bessin où ils établiront la jonction avec les troupes américaines débarquées à Omaha (1ère DI U.S.). Trois péniches LCA heurtent des obstacles, 70 hommes sont à la mer. C'est ensuite le combat de rues dans le Hamel pour conquérir la ligne de départ des 300 Commandos valides, certains ré-équipés d'armes allemandes après leurs naufrages. Dans une course contrôlée, contournant Arromanches et la batterie de Longues, ils parviennent à Escures et la falaise de Port le soir, qu'ils nettoieront le lendemain, au prix de 200 pertes en 36 heures et 300 prisonniers ennemis. Les hommes du Lieutenant-Colonel Philipps ont certainement mérité ce 6 juin, l'honneur d'appartenir aux Commandos.

The Green Berets of N°. 47 Royal Marine Commando came ashore at Hamel two hours after it was stormed by 231st Brigade and 8th Armoured Brigade, lightly armed but fatigued by the running and forced marches. Their objective was Port en Bessin, 13 kilometres from Asnelles, where they linked up with the American troops who had landed at Omaha (U.S. 1st Infantry Division). Three of the LCAs hit obstacles, throwing 70 men into the sea. Street fighting in le Hamel ensued as the remaining 300 Commandos fought to secure their start line, some having re-armed themselves with German weapons after losing their own weapons in the chaos of the landings. Bypassing Arromanches and the battery at Longues, they came to Escures and by nighttime reached the cliff at Port-en-Bessin, and mopped it up the next morning. Two hundred casualties had been sustained in 36 hours, and 300 prisoners were taken. Lieutenant-Colonel Philipps' men certainly earned the unit's pride on June 6th.

Fonds J-P. B

Les prisonniers Allemands sont utilisés à la construction de leurs propres camps provisoires, ici à Asnelles. Les « volontaires » de l'est du 642ème Bataillon n'ont eu aucune envie de combattre contre les Anglais à 7 000 km de chez eux, pour Hitler qu'ils haïssent autant que Staline, et ils ont vite capitulé. Certains se proposent pour le déminage, d'autres pour la construction des routes et il en sera tenu compte. Malheureusement pour les prisonniers ex-soviétiques, les combines politiques de la guerre froide les ramèneront en URSS où Staline les fera exécuter…

German prisoners provided the labour to build the temporary camps in which they would be held in Asnelles. The Eastern Volunteers of 642 Battalion had no desire to fight against the British, 7 000 kilometres away from home, especially for Hitler whom they despised as much as Stalin. They were among the first to surrender. Some volunteered for minesweeping, others for road-building, and they were put to work. Unfortunately for these ex-Soviet prisoners however, politics and the Cold War would force their return to the USSR where Stalin would order their execution...

Fonds J-P. B

Depuis la falaise de Saint Côme de Fresné qui culmine à 40 mètres, cette vue panoramique sur Gold Beach dans le secteur Item puis Jig, prise par un soldat allemand au début de 1944. Les obstacles de plage sont ici constitués d'éléments « C » dits portes belges, solidement ensablés et munis d'explosifs.

This panoramic view of Gold beach over Item and Jig sectors was taken from the 40-metre high cliff at Saint Côme de Fresné, by a German soldier in early 1944. The beach obstacles here are of type « C », also knows as Belgian gates, planted solidly into the sand and wired with mines.

Fonds J.-P. B / NA

Sur la falaise d'Arromanches à Saint Côme de Fresné, la station radar et son Würzburg a été mise hors d'usage par l'attaque des Typhoons de la RAF, moins de 48 heures avant l'heure-H. Le contrôle électronique de défense ennemi étant détruit, les forces du Maréchal Rommel sont aveugles à l'aube du 6 juin. Le 1ᵉʳ Hampshire y prendra 30 prisonniers résignés avant de poursuivre sur Arromanches.

On the cliff near Arromanches at Saint Côme de Fresné, the Würzburg radar installation was destroyed less than 48 hours before H-Hour by Typhoons of the Royal Air Force. With the enemy's electronic intelligence destroyed, Field Marshal Rommel's forces were blinded on the eve of June 6ᵗʰ. The 1ˢᵗ Hampshires took the surrender of 30 prisoners there, before continuing on to Arromanches.

Fonds J.-P. B

Le chaos de Saint Côme au pied de la falaise photographié en 1947 lors d'une exploration familiale. Les pontons « Whales » ont été projetés sur le roc par la tempête du 20 juin 1944, une péniche LCM y est toujours coincée, 3 ans après le débarquement ! A chaque marée, d'innombrables objets guerriers, mois après mois, viennent s'échouer en un véritable musée marin.

A chaotic state still existed at the base of the cliff at Saint Côme in 1947 and it was captured on film during this family outing. These « Whale » pontoons were beached on the rocks during the storm on June 20th 1944 and they, as well as an LCM, were still stuck there three years later. Tide after tide and month after month various military artifacts would wash ashore, creating a veritable museum on the beach.

Photo Chevrot

Arromanches libérée, 6 juin, 18 h 30

Trente prisonniers sont capturés par le 1er Hampshire de la 231ème Brigade, cela s'arrose ! Un villageois s'est avancé parmi une escouade et offre à boire, il n'a que deux verres mais le geste est sincère.

The liberation of Arromanches, June 6th, 6:30 pm

The capture of 30 enemy prisoners by Ist Battalion, the Hampshire Regiment of 231st Brigade certainly deserves a celebratory drink ! A villager came out to greet this section of soldiers and offered them a round - he only had two glasses, but the gesture was sincere.

Fonds J.-P. B

6 juin, 18 heures

La plage d'Arromanches avant l'installation du port artificiel semble bien paisible pour ses libérateurs qui la contournent par l'intérieur, depuis Le Hamel d'Asnelles.

June 6th, 6:00 pm

The beach at Arromanches, before the installation of the artificial port, must have seemed quiet to the soldiers who captured it from behind, from le Hamel at Asnelles.